Tree Verse:

A Collection of Tree Poems

John Benzee

Tree Verse: A Collection of Tree Poems

Copyright © 2017 John Benzee
Illustrations and cover art by John Benzee

All rights reserved. Except for brief passages quoted in newspaper, magazine, radio, television, or online reviews, no portion of this book may be reproduced, distributed, or transmitted in any form or by any means, electronic or mechanical, without prior written permission of the publisher.

Published by Split Seed Press
Clarence, NY
First Edition
ISBN 978-0-9997379-2-7
Visit johnbenzee.com for more info on the author

Publisher's Cataloging-In-Publication Data

Names: Benzee, John, 1995— author, illustrator.
Title: Tree verse: A collection of tree poems / by John Benzee.
Description: First edition. | Clarence : Split Seed Press, 2017.
Identifiers: ISBN 9780999737927 (paperback)
Subjects: LCSH: Trees--Poetry. | BISAC: POETRY / Subjects and
 Themes / Nature. | NATURE / Plants / Trees.
Classification: LCC PR6052.E55 T74 2017 | DDC 811.6--d23

10 9 8 7 6 5 4 3 2

I never saw a discontented tree. They grip the ground as though they liked it, and though fast rooted they travel about as far as we do. They go wandering forth in all directions with every wind, going and coming like ourselves, traveling with us around the sun two million miles a day, and through space heaven knows how fast and far!

-John Muir

Preface

This collection of fifty poems chronicles many of the diverse trees of the United States. From conifers to deciduous, trees are unique and play a special role in their distinct natural setting. Each tree presented in the poems was researched in order to incorporate a special characteristic or meaning that the tree may have. Just like a forest, which may contain changing terrain and different plant species, these poems are in no particular grouping or order. May these poems inspire you to go seek out and befriend a tree and share in Nature's tall, leafy bounty.

A Seed

A slow ticking
Clock
Dies
In the moist blanket of
Earth.

A fresh, new life,
Invisible,
Seeks
Truth among the
Sunlight.

A brown vessel
Signaled
Begin
And so it was set into
Motion.

Sapling

Not much taller than a
Deer's hind leg and
Not much thicker than a
Plump earthworm,
But young. Oh, so young.

The future of the forest,
All knobby, thin, and supple,
Seeking, ever so slowly, the last bit
Of streaming sunlight.
Try as it may, to be one of the
Special ones, who grows and grows
Past hungry teeth, sharp claws,
And nature's trying elements
To be one of the rulers of the forest.

Does the little one dream? Hope?
That it will reach its height,
Racing against its determined siblings
Scattered around.
Or, quite simply, take what it gets,
Nourishment or injury,
As it keeps on growing up.

Cherry Tree

Pretty pink petals
Pop petite perfume
Predict premature pips

Secretive smells scatter
Somber spring sneezers
Show shifting season

Beacons beckon blooms
Before blistering brilliance
Brunch bowls born

Flourish fattened fruit
Future folk feast
Favorite fabled festival

Roots regulate ripen
Renowned repeat repertoire
Rule restaurant resource

Time of the Maple Tree

When the waxy, tan cocoon
Helicoptered down a future life
Into the soft, healthy soil,
It was time.

When the welcoming water, warmth,
And humid air stirred it into motion,
Bursting up into the bright cloud sky,
It was time.

When the first mint green leaves,
Then the tenth, then the thousandth,
Then three stories tall shimmered in the breeze,
It was time.

When the sweet sap blood flowed or the
Sun-catchers changed from green to vibrant red
Or the slaying bolt of lightning struck true,
It was time.

For every solidary day,
Every present moment,
The maple tree lived, breathed,
It was time.

Oak

Once a wee little acorn,
Then a brave, young springy sprout,
The now grand old oak
Is one of the elders of the forest;
A wise great-grandparent of many others.

Deep within its solid rings
Contains intimate knowledge of
Droughts and storms, floods and feasts.
Memories too of many happenings:
The yearly proud robins and their chicks
Or the 80,000 insects with tickly feet
And the ghastly ice storm of '06.

All contained, cell upon cell,
In its creaking branches and tired trunk,
Secret, sealed, and silent.
Now assigned to watch,
To shadow.
No one, person nor plant,
May know all that our tree experienced.
Only the worn signs of the past remain
To be discovered.

Indian Tree

Nature's stubborn arrow,
A north seeker,
A life's guide,
Telling without words.

Faithful to its task,
Like the earthly celestial orbit
Or the seasons' playful schedule,
Even when forgotten and unemployed.

What may seem like a random,
Out of place branch
Was the direction home,
A usefulness fashioned from supple bark.

The Three Birches

We three birch
Are family,
Sisters to be exact,
Sprouted from our mother
During the season of falling stars.

We're unique:
One of us is tall and skinny,
Another is somewhat knobby,
And a third bends and twists,
But all still beautiful to behold.

Our entangled roots
Keep us close,
Sending nimble messages to each other:
"Hey, you have insects."
"The sun is over here."
"Quit poking me!"

Sometimes we leave anonymous
Scrolled-up notes to passersby
That peels from our sandpaper body.
We're a talkative bunch
As trees go, but
We're in the same grove,
So it's just our nature.

Life and Death of an Ash Tree

I saw you, fine ash tree
In the cold, frosty winter
Clinging beautifully onto the
Powdered snow on your spindly branches.
Strong and stately you seemed,
Able to endure all of life's weather.

Then in the spring, I saw you
Dead. No leaves, no sap, no life.
Only a worn trunk full of
Insect holes. Deadly gems of emerald
Pierced you through. Dark
Hungry mouths weakened you,
Bringing down your superiority.
No longer would you reach up
Toward the sun.

Sequoia

Do you know
How old I am?
In years,
Weeks or days?
Many moons have passed;
A bunch of incremental numbers.

So too can my size
Or my towering height
Be measured, calculated
And keenly observed.
Why? Because I
Stick out.

My records are a tightly packed,
Ringed catalog,
One within me.
I know many things
And knew many more,
But will you?
How long will you last?

Apple Tree

Everyone always thinks
Of me when the
Weather changes from
Puffy warmth to crisp sharp air.

Not when I welcome the sun
With soft white petals.
Not when I reach for the pin-pricked stars
Among the zippy mosquitos.

But when,
Laden with future offspring,
Matured to stop sign red or school bus yellow,
Many coarse hands
Pluck them from my nurtured grasp.
Then do others remember.

As the leaves tumble down,
So do my yearly gifts
To be turned into drinks, desserts,
Or eaten raw.
The apple tree— known for
What it humbly provides.

Tale of a Christmas Tree

One
Who is
Humble,
A babe (in tree years).

Not so many years ago
A gift from the mother,
Now nestled among
Comforting, swaddling snowbanks
And solitary sentinel rocks.
It stands,
Tender green branches reaching out,
To gently remind passerby of the season.

But hark!
What is that among the stars?
An axe blade among innocents!
As the little one falls,
Crown to solid earth,
The sap runs like fresh blood
To become the honored
Tree of Christmas.

Pear Tree

Every
Pear tree
Has in its nature
To give.

Plump pears in autumn
Is the standard request
From the hungry ones desiring
To satisfy their repetitious appetite.

Each year
A few more of nature's candy
Dangle and drop
For the treasure seekers
Bent on gaining a rustic meal.

Blue Spruce Forest

Colonizers
Of the inhospitable tundra.
Waxen winter coats
Brace the icy subzero winds.
Strong willed,
Where the bear and the caribou
Roam free.

Teal blue,
With a hint of green.
A prickly ocean
That softly blends in with the
Usual white eggshell landscape.

A shelter for some,
A land marker for many,
Here to show that
Trees can survive
In just about anyplace
With a little help from Mother Nature.

Black Walnut

Bam!
Miniature bowling balls
Drop down hazardously,
Solid seeds of misery.

A cursed, dangerous tree, with
Roots that force others away.
A hint of nastiness runs throughout,
A dark spell.

But to the intimidating tree
Perhaps only a coping mechanism,
A "keep away" sign
To ensure survival.

Cottonwood

Translucent,
Bleached cotton flakes
Drifting to and fro.
Summer's annual snowfall.
Beetle pillows
Surge everywhere.

Whimsical
And familiar,
To announce the sun's triumph
Over the frigid cold of winter.
A new time
To grow and to play.

Soft,
Like a lamb's ear,
Fragile,
Like a single spider's silk,
Yet able to go and be remembered.
All from one expressive family of trees.

Hickory's Strength

I can
Take a hit, a nick,
Or a strong, sudden gale.

I am
Built tough
To endure
Unexpected, unknown threats.

To keep
Alive
For future prodigy,
Our only hope.

Always
The end goal,
To persevere
With wood of solid steel.

Beech

It bears
The worn scars
Of other's words,
Of long lost love,
Passing excitement,
And promises.

Heart-shaped
Graffiti
On smooth, innocent bark.
Permanent for many years,
But ultimately gone.

What did it do to be marked?
To be used
By others to vocalize their hearts?
This life,
From leaf-top lookout,
To root cellar,
Wanted nothing more
Than to be hugged.

Hawthorn Home

Home is
Two wing beats
Past the blue grasses,
Twelve jumps from Mrs. Floppy's burrow.

No tree is ever alone
Without some kind of life,
Heartbeats and breath nearby.

Many limbs serve dual purposes:
The cardinal family with the new fluffy chicks
On the southwest branch.
Mr. Tapper's (woodpecker)
Buffet out near the old scar.
The curious ant colony,
Roving to and fro,
Nestled among the stoic roots.
Even Graytail, the squirrel,
Finds a useful lookout post once in a while.

Home,
For many beasts,
Is where the hawthorn is.

Magnolia

To come from
An ancient family line
When the world was vastly different
And to survive the
Calamities that always occur
Permits the orchestration of impressive flowers.

Yet everything,
Flowers, seeds, bark, leaves, tree,
Is never permanent.
No, not even the glacial rock
Or the leftover bones or the huge dinosaurs
Will last forever.

While trees will grow, they also will die.
The unique seed to seed code may end,
Worn down, eroded, and erased
By uncontrollable forces
Of air, water, and fire.

All is made with a nagging desire
To last forever.
Preservation is always an aim,
But for the trees,
Even the historical magnolias,
Time will run out,
Sand upon silt upon clay.

Joshua Tree

Coming close to death
Is a yearly occurrence
When the infernal oven is
Turned up so that nothing
Dares venture out until twilight
And water is a vanished dream.

Knowing how to thrive
Among malevolent sand and stone
Requires detailed planning
(Consulting the past always helps).
Patience too is vital,
To wait for that blessed day
When relief trickles down the trunk
From distant gray clouds
To get life moving again,
A resuscitation in the wild.

Dance of the Tulip Tree

Spring's showy decadence,
Filled with sweet crystal nectar,
Is mimicked in a summer flower,
A simple beacon in the treetop.

Through the countless
Waving of nimble hands that follow
The wind's ever-changing pattern,
The bees sluggishly zig-zag
To the natural pot of gold,
A rare flavor every year.

It is a guessing game
Of where the summer tulip
Will make its appearance
And when creamy yellow will burst
Forth amid tints of green.

Evergreen

To be
An evergreen
Means maintaining the
Color of life all the time.

Green means
Rich in the gift to grow.
A symbol of the family
Of unique flora,
To go towards the light.

To share the sweet scent
Of vitality and hope
Amid a dreary lifeless season.
For an evergreen is serious
—Always green.

Japanese Maple

Odd burnt red cousin
Founded own way happily
Fate keeps heartwood peace

Pine

Naturally
Eager to reach
The warm, welcoming brilliance
It has known and sought
Since its birth as a seed.

Long nimble fingers
Carry on the tradition of
Reaching, stretching out.
Poofs of moss green fireworks,
Fashioned to capture the light,
Never achieve
The principle source,
No matter its yearning
Or begging from below.

Dogwood

The dogwood is
Never in existence
Only for itself.

It provides
A safe haven,
A camouflaged shelter,
For the bushy tails
To escape the barking beasts,
Who decide that climbing
Is not for them.

Extra
Discarded branches,
It gives to any passersby
Who can pick them up,
So that tools can be fashioned
To help them reach their potential.

The dogwood
Can be the best friend
To many creatures.

Elm Row

We elm are
Loyal companions,
Arranged like soldiers in a line,
Two by two.
Our neighboring branches
Reach out for a
Leafy high-five
Amid the rustling tree tops.
Here we form
A secret passageway,
A route of seclusion,
A natural envelopment,
Away from man-made things.
Each elm contributes
To the whole,
Aiding in the vast creation
Of a trip down a gentle,
Quiet lane of memories.

Fir

Flexible forest fortification
Fundamental facile farm
Food factory fixed

Natural noble needles
Note needful network
Novel northern neighbor

Broad brittle bark
Block brutal bugs
Brown bolstered barricade

Sizeable skyward society
Solar seeking serenity
Sculpt scrambled stems

Cypress Tree

Cypress knees,
Worn from the works,
No longer soft and springy.
Familiar with the rough and the cold,
Trying to hold its ground.

Water loving—
What a deep necessity.
Standing close around,
Never out of reach,
But soaked, always wet,
Seeking the liquid silver
Vital to health.

A resting spot
For the hungry copper snake
Or the tired gray turtle
Amongst a silent, stationary friend.

Sweet Sugar Maple

Hidden gold,
A euphoria of taste,
Oozes out from an elongated treasure chest.
A tender sweetness of melted snow
And fresh crystal water,
Drip, drip, dripping
From a wild tree.

Willow

The air
I breathe in
Returns
Clean, undefiled
—A deep breath.

The water
I eagerly drink
Of bogs and wetlands
Is transformed
To unpolluted fresh water
—A refreshing drink.

The soil
I am anchored to
Is slowly purified,
As harmful wastes
Are absorbed
So that others are not injured
—Ready for new growth.

My wood is light
But my tasks are sometimes heavy,
Bearing the rejects of others.
Still, the cattails and I
Have races
To see who can
Amend our Earth the fastest.

Tropical Fruit Trees

Orange
Burnt-gold planets
Laden and stationary,
Sphere of citrus,
Soon to be squeezed.

Lemon
Parakeet yellow pieces
Of sealed tropical weather
Get sour,
Temperamental fruit.

Lime
Portioned tropical prairies
In tangy green orbs
Content in the blazing heat,
Reflect Nature's favorite hue.

Holly

Bright, blood red berries,
Proclamations of truth,
That in the darkness of the low sun
There will soon be new light.
That the barrenness of the present moment
Will not last;
New life will arise,
Hope will be born again.

Prickly thorns
Encircle the red,
A ring of hurt for those who dare
Take, without permission.
A mother, guarding her young.
A king, guarding his castle.

For when the two
Amid verdant green pasture,
Above a pure white backdrop,
Say "Noel",
The cold, icy grip
Will not last forever.

Palm Tree

Prepared for summer fun
A carnival outdoors
Blowing in the breeze
Unstill, never stationary.

Ready for the sun's stifling heat
For the long hours called day
Important for growth,
But sometimes too extreme.

Armored deep,
With ship's mast trunk
All set for the surprise hurricane,
Eager to show true strength.

Aspen Melody

As the gentle breeze blows
Down the still mountain
Tapping, ever so slightly
The golden leaves, now past their peak,
A single whisper echoes forth.
More rustles slowly follow
As the breath of air rises.
Soon a twinkling tree melody resonates,
The first performance of autumn,
A serenade to summer's end.
The leaves quake to give
Honor to the long forgotten
Heroes of the age.
A primitive, but catching tune
Fit for man and beast,
Who hear and journey forth,
A new song close to their heart.

Mahogany

Some trees wonder
About their future,
Their personal afterlife.
When being a tree means
Coming to the twilight of life.
Instead, certain parts must remain,
Such as the rings of wood,
Grown steadily from the soil and air.
Some dream to be played
At notable concert halls,
Producing a sweet harmony
As instruments of man's restless fingers.
Others ponder the next life
Of supporting a royal king's back
Or serving the finest fruit
To a group of faithful friends.
Each mahogany tree
Will have a future.
Its place will be somewhere
After being cut down and transformed.
Where, is the question,
And the answer, still unknown,
But it is still trying to be the best,
Knowing it will have value.

Sycamore Yellow

Approaching frost heralds in
A new color, brighter than traditional green.
Darker than a daisy's center spot,
Lighter than mustard's flower.
A more golden yellow,
Remembering the source of light
That danced along its absorbent leaves,
But now a splash of color against
The rain soaked clouds.

A strong yellow
To signal inner strength that will continue.
A sharp yellow, like aged cheese,
To announce its loyal protection of the field.
A yellow that appears
When green is lost,
But by no means causes sadness
Or a loss of decorum,
But only the regal reach of
Nimble branches, holding pin-shaped stems
Of yellow flags for honored sunshine.

Ginkgo

We ginkgo trees
Are often alone
With no close living relatives
To relate to
Or share secret knowledge
Of what it means
To be a ginkgo.

We must
Press on
Leaf upon leaf,
Root upon root,
To make the best of
Our present circumstances,
Which is why we have a few
Tricks up our bark.
Aerial roots sneak out
To grab excess moisture
And even begin a new tree,
All in the name of ginkgo.

Poplar

It knows the ancient customs
Encircling the trampled ground
Where natural discourse is held
In close communion.
It holds the rhythm of many voices
Deep in its heartwood.

The people's tree,
Fit to make allowances
And bear the necessary burdens.
The flexible interior
Can go along with changing pressures,
In order to hold honorable leaves up high.
Deep rooted, it brings significance,
And another use to an empty, unnamed spot
Where people gather.

Chestnut Tree

Some trees are known
For what they provide,
As if the seasonal gift
Is more important than the giver.

The chestnut tree is one example.
For the sweet nuts it duly provides,
To be roasted and snacked upon
Before winter's deep sleep,
Bear the recognition.
The tree, grown from one of these
Preserved nuts that escaped the open fire,
Has stately grown to an enormous size,
Capable of providing fodder
For squirrels and humans alike.

It is the mighty tree,
Dormant in winter's blanketed embrace,
That should be thanked
For its hard work and dedication
To its craft.

Juniper

Longevity runs in the family.
The ability to stay alive,
Through trying circumstances,
To tell the vivid stories of
Days of past fidelity.

Small blue marbles
Are a continued decoration
And a sign of strength.
To play the game of chance
So that one berry may fall to the ground,
Be buried, and develop
Into a faithful offspring,
Fit to carry on the family name.

Yew

Beware the witching hour
When fairy sprite
And faun and satyr gather,
And power is sought among
Wood that has tapped into
The unchecked potential
Of ancient unseen forces below.

Yet the intentions are good
To ward evil away,
Like water and oil, and
Let the good flourish under the shade.
Hedged in by many-leafed branches
Entwined together to form a secure screen,
Closely guarding the secrets of the little ones,
Those who are looked down upon
And deemed insignificant.

Weeping Willow

A frozen waterfall
Of individual currents suspended
In slow motion,
Stretching towards the ground,
A wide open bucket.

Tanned hair, of many strands,
Shyly hiding the face
That then blows secretively in the breeze
To reveal a hidden mystery.

Dangling knotted rope,
Swinging for some creature,
A rough pathway to the top
Where a new adventure awaits by ship.

For the weeping that is always present
Is either from sadness,
Bringing forth tears that seek for water
Or a cry of joy, of passionate delight
That overwhelms, and the gleeful expression
Can be captured in a stationary stance
Suspended for all to see.

Alder Line

A living marker of boundaries
Where earth meets flowing water
And different niches lend to diverse living beings
Capable of thriving in their special spot,
A perimeter marking new beginnings.

A boundary to teach
The ways of life in storied rhyme
As fabled folk learn their ways
Or a border that keeps secure,
So stress can float away
And a confined haven is properly sought.

Even the wood, built to last,
Maintains its hard resistance to
The typical means of recycling by watery rot,
To prolong the inevitable end.

Plum Tree

Styled for the formal spring ball,
With calm pink petals dressing elegant branches,
Serenaded by happy crickets and lonely frogs
Eager to celebrate another year.

Purple, a favorite color,
Is mixed on tart fruit
Flowing with juices fit for a queen,
Yet a hard inner stone remains,
A balance of what is edible
And what is tossed away, uneaten.
Both halves serve their purpose
Along the short waltz of nature's time.

Sassafras Tree

Deep root,
Tapped into fertile ground,
Sucks up cool water
Bubbling and gurgling through
The pipe network,
Mixed with sweet, aromatic flavor
To provide a thirst quenching drink,
Brewed for all.

Linden Love

Proclaiming its love
Faithfully every year
On quaint leaves attired in happy green,
To the one who awakens
And calls forth from the sleepy buds,
To form heart-shaped leaves
In affection for the bright
Shining bulb high in the sky.

The joy of being cared for
Is shared with the wide world
In sweet smells of lazy flowers
That perfume the air, making everything aware
Of the linden's love of the sun.

Boxelder Shade

As the school bell tolls
In anticipated note
And the boisterous school children,
Brains overflowing with useful knowledge,
Spill out into the warm world,
The boxelder stands tall,
Marking the school grounds.

Every swinging leaf, arrayed in a line,
Shades the flattened ground below
For kids to rest and learn in comfort,
Sheltered from the harsh rays of surging light.

A relaxing place is the best
For friendly conversations, intriguing debates
And even a serious game or two
Underneath many blurry shadows
Filtering dancing sunlight.

Hornbeam

A sprawling ladder,
Leading to a good view,
Cylindrical steps
With random bumps and curves
Offer an easy way to the top,
Able to take the trying weight.
It has worked out,
Through rain and wind, over the years
To be called "Musclewood."
Strong and sturdy like a ship's main mast,
Providing a key lookout point and
A crow's nest with a clear view
Over the shrunken landscape below.

Hemlock

Log cabin home
Drilled into wood
Four decades old.
New lives living
In a tired tree.
Little clawed feet scour the bark,
Searching for the juiciest insect
And tap, tap, tapping
With miniature jack hammers
For the next snack.
Mulch shards fly
As the hunt progresses.
The crawly itch ceases
And an empty belly is filled.

Log

No longer part of a whole,
A splintered division,
Weakened and softened by the elements,
Slowly breaking down
Into rich fragments,
Returning to what it once was.
Cracked bones devoid of life,
Now in another transformation process,
Whittled down from majestic heights
To scattered, hollow woodchips.

Index of trees:

Alder, 44
Apple, 11
Ash, 9
Aspen, 35
Beech, 18
Birch, 8
Boxelder, 48
Cherry, 4
Chestnut, 40
Christmas, 12
Cottonwood, 6
Cypress, 29
Dogwood, 26
Elm, 27
Evergreen, 23
Fir, 28
Ginkgo, 38
Hawthorn, 19
Hemlock, 50
Hickory, 17
Holly, 33
Hornbeam, 49
Indian, 7
Joshua, 21
Juniper, 41
Linden, 47
Log, 51
Magnolia, 20
Mahogany, 36
Maple, 5
   Japanese, 24
   Sugar, 30

Oak, 6
Palm, 34
Pear, 13
Pine, 25
Plum, 45
Poplar, 39
Sapling, 3
Sassafras, 46
Seed, 2
Sequoia, 10
Spruce, 14
Sycamore, 37
Tropical fruit, 32
Tulip, 22
Walnut, black, 15
Willow, 31
   Weeping, 43
Yew, 42

www.ingramcontent.com/pod-product-compliance
Lightning Source LLC
Chambersburg PA
CBHW030303030426
42336CB00009B/499